Contents

A a

ax

Annie Ant

Color the letter a. Say the "**a**" sound.

  Say the words. Trace the line to help Annie find the ax.

ant

ax

B b

ball

Benny Bear

Color the letter b. Say the "**b**" sound.

  Say the words. Color the ball.

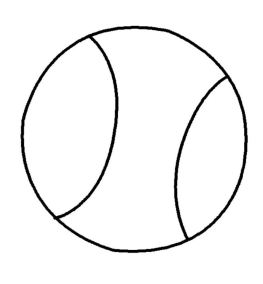

bear

ball

C c

cut

Candy Cat

Circle the letters **c**. Say the "**c**" sound.

  Listen carefully. Place the correct sticker in the box.

D d

dig

Danny Dog

Color the letter d. Say the "**d**" sound.

 Circle the animals with the letter "**d**."

E e

egg

Eddie Elephant

Trace the line to help the hen find her egg.
Say the "e" sound.

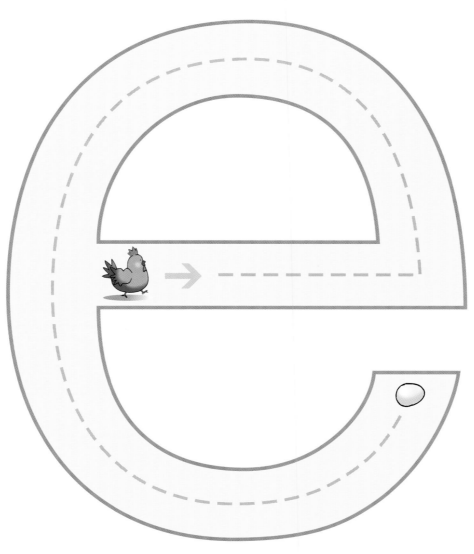

Listen carefully. Circle the correct words and pictures.

egg    dog

cat   elephant

F f

fin

Fanny Fish

Circle the letters **f**. Say the "**f**" sound.

  Say the word. Color the **f**ish.

fish

Circle the letters a, b, c, d, e and f. Say the sounds.

Join the words that begin with the same sound.

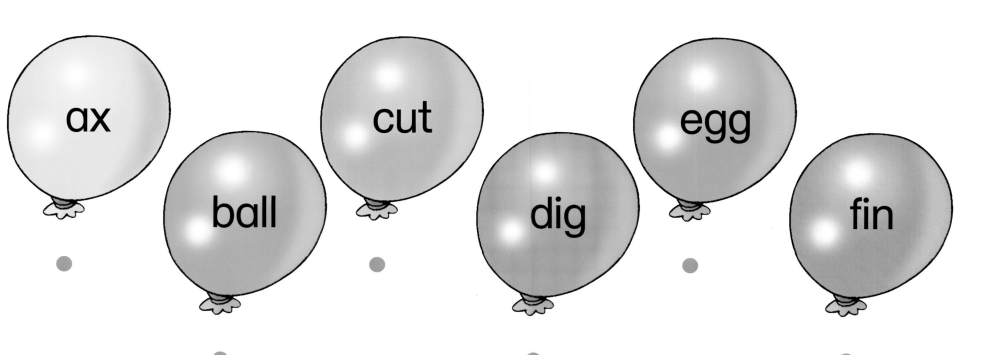

ax ball cut dig egg fin

cat ant elephant bear fish dog

G g

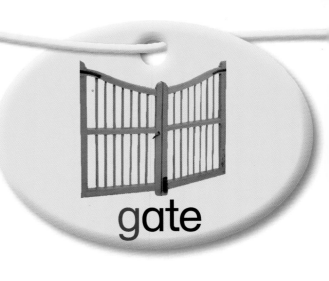

gate

Goldie Goose

Phonics for Kids   Book I

P.7

cut   cat

P.19

hat   hen

P.29

monkey   mouth

Color the letter g. Say the "**g**" sound.

  Say the words. Match the words with the correct pictures.

goose •

•

gate •

•

Hh

hat

Henna Hen

Color the letter h. Say the "h" sound.

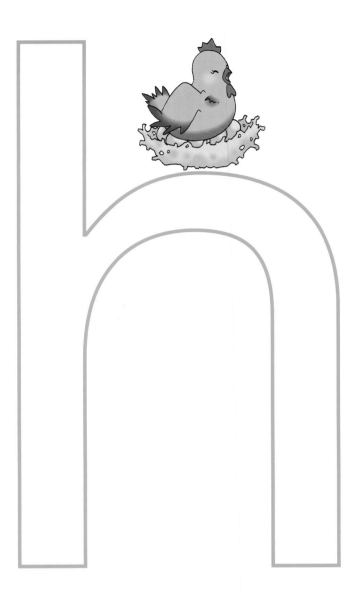

  Listen carefully. Place the correct sticker in the box.

19

I i

ill

Ian Insect

Color the letter i. Say the "i" sound.

 Join the dots. Say the word.

insect

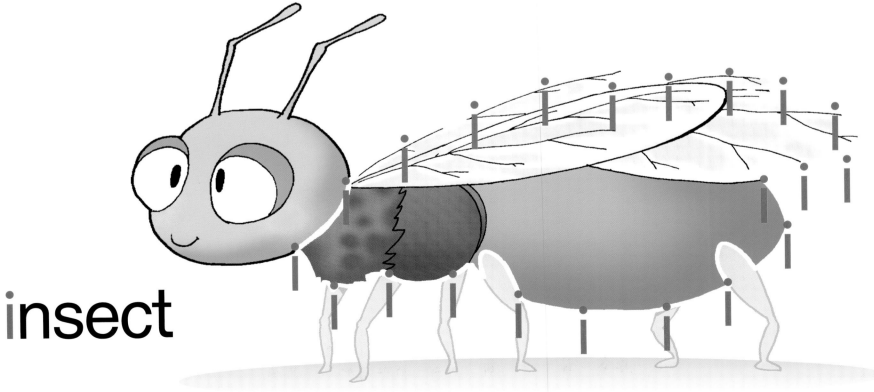

J j

jump

Jane Jellyfish

Circle the letters **j**. Say the "**j**" sound.

  Say the word. Check the correct picture.

jump

K k

kick

Kenny Kangaroo

  Trace the line to help Kenny find the ball. Say the "**k**" sound.

  Listen carefully. Circle the correct words.

kick

kangaroo

hen

L l

leg

Larry Lion

Circle the letters **l**. Say the "**l**" sound.

  Trace the line. Say the word.

leg

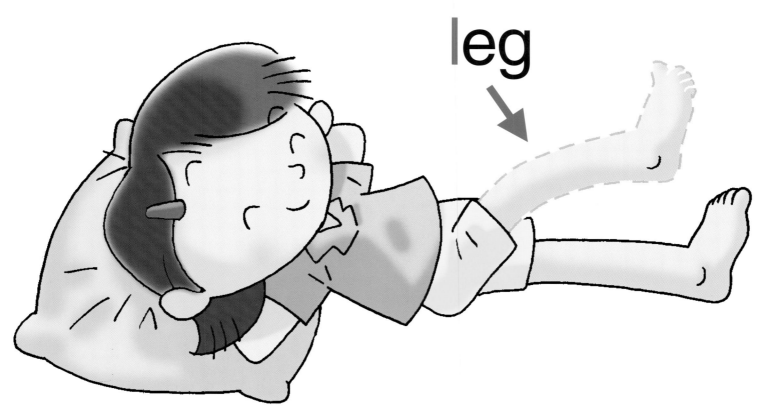

M m

mouth

Micky Monkey

Color the letter m. Say the "m" sound.

 Listen carefully. Place the correct sticker in the box.

Listen carefully. Circle the correct pictures.

g

h

i

j

k

l

m